An Internet timeline

1822

Charles Babbage starts to design the first programmable computer, his Difference Engine.

1963

First use of ASCII code to represent characters as numbers that computers can read.

1971

The first email message is sent, by Ray Tomlinson. He's forgotten what it said!

1866

First radio transmission of Morse code.

1969

First message sent on the ARPAnet, which came before the Internet.

1944

Colossus, the first digital, electronic, programmable computer, starts work at Bletchley Park, England, cracking German war codes.

1999
The first popular smartphones are released, making the Internet available to people on the move.

1989
Tim Berners-Lee proposes the World Wide Web.

2005
Google Earth provides free, scalable mapping of the whole world over the Internet.

1993
Web browser Mosaic brings the Web to everyone.

2015
A spanner is 3D-printed on the International Space Station, using a file emailed from Earth.

1977
The Apple II becomes the first mass-market personal computer.

2004
Approximate start of 'Web 2.0', which lets users build their own Web content.

Internet use around the world

Percentage of people with Internet access on each continent.

Lowest *Highest*

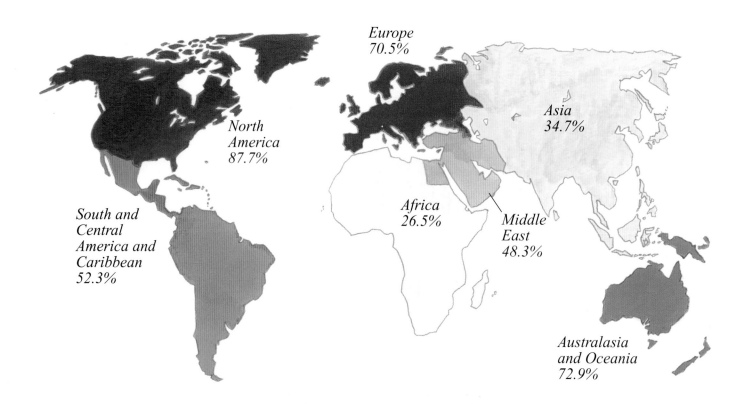

Europe
70.5%

Asia
34.7%

North
America
87.7%

Africa
26.5%

Middle
East
48.3%

South and
Central
America and
Caribbean
52.3%

Australasia
and Oceania
72.9%

How many people use the Internet where you live?

In Asia, 1.386 billion people use the Internet. But that's only a third (34.7%) of Asia's huge population.

In North America, 87.7% of the population uses the Internet, or 310 million people.

In Europe, 70.5% of the population (nearly three out of four) uses the Internet; that comes to 582 million people.

In Australasia and Oceania, 72.9% of people (26.8 million) use the Internet. The Middle East has 112 million users. South and Central America, including the Caribbean, have 320 million between them.

The lowest level of Internet use at present is in Africa, where only one in four people has access to the Internet. That's 26.5% of the population, or 298 million people.

(Figures correct as of 2014)

Author:

Anne Rooney studied English at Cambridge University, England, and then earned a Ph.D. at Cambridge. She has held teaching posts at several UK universities and is currently a Royal Literary Fund fellow at Newnham College, Cambridge. She has written more than 150 books for children and adults, including several on the history of science and medicine. She also writes children's fiction.

Artist:

Mark Bergin was born in Hastings, England, in 1961. He studied at Eastbourne College of Art and has specialised in historical reconstructions as well as aviation and maritime subjects since 1983. He lives in Bexhill-on-Sea, England, with his wife and three children.

Series creator:

David Salariya was born in Dundee, Scotland. He has illustrated a wide range of books and has created and designed many new series for publishers in the UK and overseas. David established The Salariya Book Company in 1989. He lives in Brighton, England, with his wife, illustrator Shirley Willis, and their son Jonathan.

Editor: **Stephen Haynes**

Editorial Assistants: **Mark Williams, Rob Walker**

Cover artwork: **David Antram**

Published in Great Britain in MMXVI by Book House, an imprint of
The Salariya Book Company Ltd
25 Marlborough Place, Brighton BN1 1UB
www.salariya.com
www.book-house.co.uk
ISBN: 978-1-910184-92-9

S A L A R I Y A

1 3 5 7 9 8 6 4 2

A CIP catalogue record for this book is available from the British Library.

Printed and bound in China.

Visit our website at **www.book-house.co.uk**
or go to **www.salariya.com** for **free** electronic versions of:
You Wouldn't Want to be an Egyptian Mummy!
You Wouldn't Want to be a Roman Gladiator!
You Wouldn't Want to be a Polar Explorer!
You Wouldn't Want to sail on a 19th-Century Whaling Ship!

PAPER FROM
SUSTAINABLE
FORESTS

You Wouldn't Want to Live Without™

The Internet!

Written by
Anne Rooney

Illustrated by
Mark Bergin

Series created by
David Salariya

BOOK HOUSE
a SALARIYA *imprint*

Contents

Introduction

Where do you go if you want to know what an aardvark looks like, how to make a kaleidoscope, or which planet or moon is most likely to be home to aliens? Probably online!

Over the last 20 years the Internet – and especially the World Wide Web – has become the first place we look for information. And we don't head online just to find things out. We watch videos, catch up on TV programmes, keep in touch, go shopping, hang out with friends, show off our photos, and a host of other things. We're online from our computers, laptops, tablets, phones and even watches. Could you live without the Internet? Would you want to? Do you dare to try?

Online safety

Before you go online, read page 33 for tips on how to stay safe.

Don't worry: you can still use books!

What exactly is the Internet?

The Internet and the Web – what's the difference? It's easy to mix them up. The Internet is a physical network of connected computers; the Web is a vast set of linked files kept on those computers. As we share, copy, view and move information, the network buzzes with activity. It's never off, never quiet – and sometimes parts of it are so overloaded that everything slows down, like a massive data traffic jam.

The Internet isn't only home to the Web. Data of all kinds moves around over the Internet. Every time you send an email or an instant message, store a file in cloud storage, or play an online game on your console, you're using the Internet.

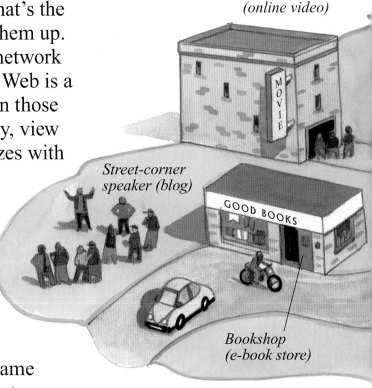

Cinema (online video)

Street-corner speaker (blog)

GOOD BOOKS

Bookshop (e-book store)

TO MOVE around the Internet, information is changed to strings of numbers. It's changed back to meaningful information by the computer at the other end – you never see the numbers.

JUST LIKE a traffic highway, the Internet has a choice of different routes to every place. Sometimes it's super-busy!

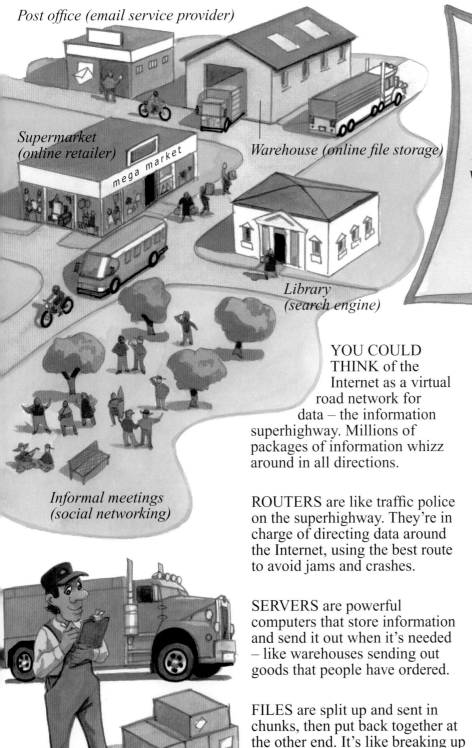

Post office (email service provider)

Supermarket
(online retailer)

mega market

Warehouse (online file storage)

Library
(search engine)

Informal meetings
(social networking)

The Internet links computers using wires and radio waves. At home, you have a modem that plugs into the cable network that runs underground. Your phone, tablet and other items communicate with the modem wirelessly, using radio waves.

YOU COULD THINK of the Internet as a virtual road network for data – the information superhighway. Millions of packages of information whizz around in all directions.

ROUTERS are like traffic police on the superhighway. They're in charge of directing data around the Internet, using the best route to avoid jams and crashes.

SERVERS are powerful computers that store information and send it out when it's needed – like warehouses sending out goods that people have ordered.

FILES are split up and sent in chunks, then put back together at the other end. It's like breaking up a jigsaw puzzle and mailing the parts separately to a friend.

What can you do on the Internet?

You can use the Internet almost anywhere, from the top of a mountain to a ship in the middle of the ocean – as long as you have one of the billions of Internet-enabled devices in the world.

We've all grown dependent on the Internet very quickly. We rely on it for entertainment, communication, shopping, banking, healthcare, news, government – all the things that keep our societies running smoothly. In fact, it's more a question of what *can't* you do on the Internet!

YOU CAN BUY almost anything online, from a meteorite to a tiger (check with a parent first). Most people settle for books, games, clothes, food, travel and music.

Brilliant! Something for everyone!

WHAT DO YOU LIKE to watch or listen to? Whatever you like, you'll find it somewhere online. Baby sloths playing? There's a webcam for that. Mongolian throat singing? No problem. Missed your favourite programme last week? The Internet is your time machine!

You can do it!

How many Internet-connected devices do you have at home? Computer, laptop, tablet, phone, game console? Make a list. What do you use them all for? Do you use each one differently?

YOU CAN PLAY online games on your own, with friends down the road, or even with people on the other side of the world.

IF YOU WANT to learn something your school doesn't teach – like Inuit or guitar-playing – there will be lessons online. Or you can go online for help with your homework.

Hi, Gramps!

YOU CAN CHAT to friends and family anywhere in the world online. Or use blogging and microblogging sites to share your interests with everyone.

DOES NO-ONE BELIEVE your dog can skateboard? Post a video on a social media or file-sharing page and they can see for themselves!

How did we share information before?

The world wasn't an information vacuum before the Internet. People have been talking for thousands of years. Then we started writing – that made it possible to communicate with someone who wasn't right there with you. Printing made that even easier. Then we developed radio and television and it was possible to see and hear someone far away. We can even watch live videos from space and other planets now – communications have come a long way.

READING really took off after Johannes Gutenberg made the first European printing press, about 1450. Suddenly, books were everywhere.

Screw for pressing down the platen

Compositors assembling the type

Printer removing printed pages

Printer inking the type

Platen

THE EARLIEST WRITING was pressed into clay tablets with a special stick called a stylus. That was in ancient Sumer more than 5,000 years ago. And now we've gone right back to writing on tablets with a stylus!

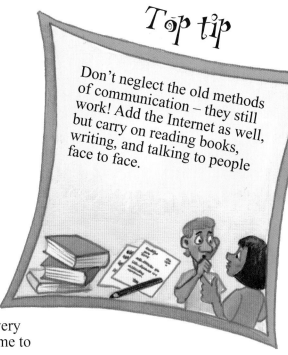

Top tip

Don't neglect the old methods of communication – they still work! Add the Internet as well, but carry on reading books, writing, and talking to people face to face.

FOR CENTURIES, people wrote with a quill pen that had to be dipped into ink every few words. It took a long time to write out a whole book.

RADIO (below left) was invented in 1866 but at first it was only used for Morse code – letters coded in dots and dashes. The first voice broadcast was in 1906, in Massachusetts, USA.

TELEVISION has only been around since the 1920s, and it was all black and white at first.

THE FIRST MOVABLE TYPE was made in China about 1,000 years ago. Chinese writing has thousands of characters. Printers used a separate wooden block for each one.

The geeks are coming!

Imagine how long it would take if you had to do every calculation by hand. That's why people invented automatic calculating machines. Even having to tell the machine exactly what to do each time was a bore. The answer was programming – preparing a list of instructions for the machine to follow and letting it get on with the job.

The first programmable machine was a loom for weaving patterns into fabric. Now, lots of machines can do things on their own, controlled by computers and programming – still including looms.

It's amazingly accurate.

TEENAGERS have always been geeks. Blaise Pascal was only 19 when he started work on the first mechanical calculator, called the 'Pascaline', in 1642.

CHARLES BABBAGE had bigger ideas. He designed the first programmable computer, or Difference Engine, in the 1820s. Sadly, he couldn't raise the money to build it. It was finally constructed in 2002 at London's Science Museum. The Difference Engine is mechanical – it does not use electricity.

'Chain' of punched cards

A program is a long list of instructions for a computer to follow. A web browser has around 50 million instructions – it would fill 900,000 pages if you printed it out.

Uh-oh!

IN 1801 the Jacquard loom followed programs coded as holes punched in card. Early electronic computers did the same.

CODEBREAKING goes back to the start of computing. The first programmable computer that was actually built was Colossus (right), made at Bletchley Park, England, to crack German codes in the Second World War.

THE FIRST personal computer, the Altair 8800, had no screen, keyboard or mouse – just lights and switches. No videos then!

MATHEMATICAL WHIZZ KID Ada Lovelace wrote programs for Babbage's machine, but they were never tested.

A MOUSE and a desktop are now the standard way of using a computer. They first appeared on a computer called the Lisa in 1983.

13

Where did the Internet come from?

Everything starts small. The Internet began in 1969 as ARPAnet, linking just four American universities. It was used to share research, and would provide an emergency means of communication if a war or a natural disaster wiped out other methods.

It grew slowly at first, with all the linked computers in universities or research laboratories on little local networks. Because it linked these separate networks into a single interconnected network, it became known as the Internet.

Now it spans the world and even reaches out into space!

EMAIL was first used in 1971, and really took off: 75% of ARPAnet traffic was email by 1973. Now we send about 206 billion emails every day – and around 75% of that is junk mail.

West Coast universities

ARPAnet

East Coast universities

WHAT DO YOU DO on a snow day? In 1978, Ward Christensen spent his snow day building CBBS, a bulletin-board system that let people post messages online.

BLOGS and social networking started in 1980 with Usenet, a news-sharing system that allows groups of members to post themed threads of messages.

Coffee's ready – let's go!

Sure!

WEBCAMS are great for watching playing pandas or roving rovers on Mars. The very first webcam was trained on a coffee pot at Cambridge University, England.

Top tip

In 1983, users were tricked into downloading the virus ARF-ARF which deleted all their files. Check that your devices are all protected against modern online nasties.

Aaargh!

GETTING AHEAD. British queen Elizabeth II became the first national leader to send an email, in 1976.

USE SWORD

STAYING UP LATE gaming isn't new. The first games were text-only adventures, often involving knights, warriors and dragons (and a lot of typing).

ASTRONAUT John Glenn spent his 77th birthday on the space shuttle *Discovery*. US president Bill Clinton sent him a 'Happy Birthday' email into space.

IMAGINE if you had to keep your tablet and phone plugged in to use them! Luckily, they use radio waves to connect. But early computers all used cables.

15

Weaving the Web

The World Wide Web is central to our lives today – but it nearly didn't happen!

It was invented by British scientist Tim Berners-Lee, who was working at CERN in Switzerland and wanted to share files easily with his colleagues around the world. In 1989, he came up with an idea for linked pages of information kept on different networked computers, and asked if he could develop it. His boss wasn't keen. He said Berners-Lee could do it in his own time, but that it wasn't worth CERN taking on as his idea was too vague.

WEB PAGES are pretty useless if you can't look at them. Berners-Lee made a browser to display his web pages at CERN. The browser which made the Web popular with the public was Mosaic, invented by Marc Andreessen and his team and released in 1993.

You can do it!

As a child, Tim Berners-Lee made toy computers from old boxes. Make your own fantasy computer from cardboard. What will it be able to do?

THE VERY FIRST Web page, in 1991, was rather dull (above): no dancing pandas then. It was just a list of text links to all the other 25 Web pages. There are now nearly 1 billion pages on the Web.

FINDING FAVOURITE BANDS online is as old as the Web. The very first photo on a web page was of the girl band Les Horribles Cernettes. It was posted in 1992.

THE FIRST SEARCH ENGINE appeared in 1994. Before that there were lists and directories. But it was like looking for a single page in a vast library!

Web 2.0: It's a two-way thing

At first, the Web worked in one direction, like TV and radio: professionals put information and pictures and videos on the Web, and we could look at it. But now everyone can join in. The Web has become more interactive. It's called 'Web 2.0' and it lets us all upload and share files and photos. You can write a blog, share your videos, add to a wiki article, comment on a news story or even make your own web site. *See page 33 for tips about staying safe online.*

EVERYONE'S a TV station! If you see something amazing, you can share it immediately by uploading a picture or a video. And if you can't get out to the South Pole yourself, at least you can enjoy the amazing things that other people have posted.

And it's all happening right now!

18

I can tell the government what I think!

What are you really, really interested in? Dolphins? Music? Cars? Search online – and go beyond the first page of results to find some super sites, groups and blogs to follow.

WEB 2.0 is open to everyone. People who live far from cities can now follow important issues and take part in international debates. It's a chance of power for ordinary people!

SOCIAL NETWORKING means you can keep up with what your friends are doing no matter where they – or you – live.

WANT TO BE a dancer or a musician? Start now! Film your talented self and start your career as an online star.

I'm not the only octopus knitter!

EVEN the oddest hobbies have a home online. The whole world's out there – you'll find other people who like what you like.

WHATEVER problem you have, there are other people to share it with and professionals who can help or advise you.

Are you being **BULLIED?**

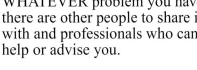

19

Information overload!

You can find out about anything on the Web, as long as you know how to look for it. It's like the best library in the history of the world, it's free, you don't need a library card, and it's in your own home (or phone!). The snag is that *anyone* can put information online. Some of it is really valuable, and some is total rubbish – it can even be dangerously wrong.

THE WEB grows and grows all the time. By 2010, we were adding as much information to the Web every two days as was added in the whole of 2002. You can never keep up with it all, so you need really good search skills to find what you need.

Programs called robotic spiders 'crawl' the Web gathering information about what's on different web pages. This is built into a vast index — and that's where a search engine looks when you search.

WHATEVER you want to know, someone will have made a web site about it. With pictures and videos, it's easy to follow instructions. And you can replay them again and again. Most teachers don't have a repeat button!

ALIEN INVASION? You'll find out on the Web first. News spreads superfast online and can be updated instantly.

CITIZEN JOURNALISTS are ordinary people reporting online about big events (right). You can do it yourself! Now we've got everything covered.

Definitely something wrong with this recipe!

COMMON SENSE. If the information doesn't *look* right, don't trust it! Check other sources to see if they agree.

EVEN if you live miles from anywhere (below), the Web can be a vast school at your fingertips!

It's a virtual world

There's another whole world (or even many worlds) inside the World Wide Web – a virtual world. You can immerse yourself in games set in imaginary realms, and learn (safely!) in a virtual environment. In real life you can't just cut people up to see what's inside, learn to fly a plane, rule an empire in ancient Egypt or run your own island. But you can do them all online.

It's not just fun and games, either. Pilots can practise landing at real airports thousands of kilometres away, and surgeons can operate on real patients through a computer screen and a robot.

Now let's see what's inside here...

VIRTUAL CURRENCIES let you pay online – often for virtual goods, like food for your monster pet. Beware of real overspending!

LEARN real skills in a virtual world. Trainee doctors can now explore the inside of a human body without cutting it up.

Remember there's a real world out there, too! Take a break from playing and learning in the virtual world to get outside and move around – it's good for you.

FLYING a virtual plane is the next best thing to flying a real one. You can learn all the skills of piloting without risking any lives. Even real pilots learn in flight simulators first (left) before they're let loose on real planes and people.

Time to take a break!

ROBOTIC SURGERY machines can be controlled by real surgeons from near or far – useful for accidents at sea or in space.

KEEP YOUR COOL – virtual mishaps can make you really angry. Too many violent computer games might be bad for you.

Sharing – whether you want to or not

The Internet started off because researchers wanted to share information. Now we can – and do – share almost everything. We share what we're doing on social networks, share our photos and videos. Lots of information about us is held online by healthcare providers, schools and governments, and shared with others who need it. Someone is always keeping an eye on us. Has it gone too far?

Sharing is good – but not *too* much sharing. We need privacy as well. You've probably done things you wouldn't want to share. Who owns information about you, and who's allowed to see it?

SHARING photos with friends and family is great. Make sure you understand privacy settings to keep your pictures secure.

IF YOU HAVE an accident, the Internet allows paramedics to check health information on the spot. It could save your life.

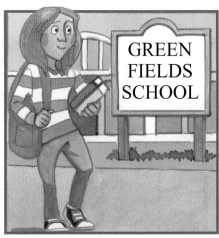

TAKE CARE of what your photos show – don't give away clues to where you live or go to school. Look after yourself online to look after yourself in the real world.

GREEN FIELDS SCHOOL

ONCE THAT PHOTO of you in your jellyfish hat is online, you can't get it back – so be careful what you share. Never post photos of others without their permission. What looks like a laugh to you might not seem funny to them.

THE WEB remembers what you look at and shares it with advertisers. You may be bombarded with adverts for things you might like – but also for some things you don't like or already have.

FOLLOW US ONLINE!

SHARING online is a good way of showing people what you can do. Some bands give away tracks to advertise their real-world gigs.

WHO'S LOOKING? Governments monitor online activity. They say it helps fight crime and keep us all safe. But some people call it snooping.

Uh-oh! I should have paid for it.

THERE'S ANOTHER good reason not to download pirated content: illegal downloads often contain viruses that may damage your files or your computer.

A global village

It's been called a 'wired world' and the 'global village' – the Internet connects people everywhere, shrinking the world so that we're all neighbours. You can see the weather on a beach in Australia while you sit in your bedroom in Europe or the United States. Someone in China can chat with a friend in Peru. You can campaign to save rhinos or supply water to a remote village. It's as quick to see something the other side of the world as something outside your window. The Internet can bring us all closer.

SEEING how other people live can make us more tolerant. We're less likely to believe propaganda about other groups if we see and interact with those people online. It's hard to hate someone you've compared fish photos with.

Many Amazonian Indians have access to the Internet.

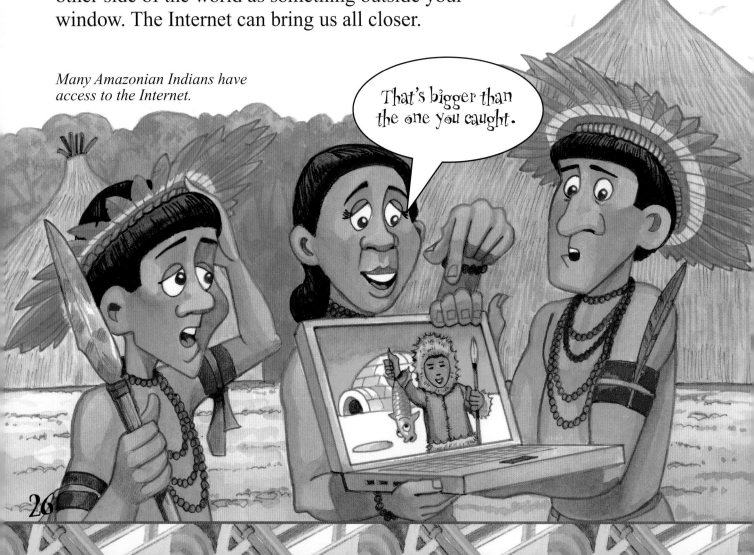

That's bigger than the one you caught.

26

NOW EVERYONE can upload photos, it's hard to keep things secret, including the bad things that happen in some places. Here's to a fairer, safer world!

ORDINARY people everywhere share their experiences. If there's no TV camera around, it doesn't matter – there will be someone with a smartphone (below).

Have you looked online?

We haven't got a computer.

AS MORE THINGS happen online, people without the Internet lose out. It's harder to get information and take part in what's going on in the world.

THE INTERNET means campaigns can be global. People on the other side of the world can help causes they would never have heard of before the Internet.

You can do it!

Find an online campaign for a cause you care about, and do something to help it. If there isn't one, start your own. You can make a difference!

SELLERS give online discounts, so people who don't have access to the Internet may miss out on the best deals and end up paying more for things.

50% off!

27

So – would you want to live without the Internet?

f the Internet were turned off tomorrow, the world would fall into chaos – banking, the emergency services, healthcare, education, entertainment, and even getting food into shops all depend on the Internet now. Yet only 40 years ago, it was used by just a few people for business and research.

The next big thing is likely to be the 'Internet of things' (IoT), in which more and more ordinary devices are connected to the Internet. Examples might include cars, home thermostats and security systems. Industry experts predict there could be 50 billion things of all types online by 2020. With the Internet running everything, we really wouldn't want to live without it!

Welcome home! Your dinner is ready. ♥

HOW ABOUT a fridge that orders food when you run out? Could the future see kitchens that never run out of milk, and the end of physical supermarkets?

WEARABLE COMPUTERS can upload information about your activity and state of health. Are they just gadgets for fitness fanatics, or could they catch on?

WIRED houses can pretty much run themselves. They can turn on the heating when you're on your way home, and turn the lights off when you go out. It's not just fun – it saves energy, so it's good for the planet, too.

Access denied

SOME people have to live without the Internet. In some countries it's banned, as leaders don't want their citizens to see how people live elsewhere.

THE INTERNET extends into space now. The Deep Space Network communicates with faraway spacecraft. Some craft even have their own social networking pages!

Glossary

3D printing Building a physical object in plastic or another material from a file sent from a computer to a 3D printer.

ARPAnet The early network of computers in the United States which later developed into the Internet.

Browser A program for displaying and interacting with web pages.

Bulletin board (or **web forum**) A web site that allows people to post and respond to notices or news items in threads (themed discussions).

CERN European Organization for Nuclear Research (Geneva, Switzerland).

Cloud storage Keeping files on a remote server connected to the Internet, instead of a hard disk or local network drive.

Data Raw information, including facts, figures, pictures, sound or video.

File A document stored on a computer, such as a text document, a picture, a spreadsheet or a video clip.

Internet-enabled device Any device that can access the Internet, including computers, smartphones and webcams.

Microblog A blogging platform that allows only very short updates, often less than 200 characters.

Modem A device which connects a computer (or a wireless network) to the Internet.

Monitor (verb) To keep watch over or keep track of something.

Movable type An old printing technology in which each character is printed from a separate small block of metal or wood. Once the page has been printed, the type can be taken apart, reassembled and used to print something else.

Online Connected to or available on the Internet.

Paramedic A healthcare professional who specialises in immediate care in an emergency.

Platen The flat plate in a printing press that presses the paper against the inked printing block.

Program A set of instructions written in computer code that tells a computer what to do. Some programs are very long and complicated, such as image-processing programs and web browsers.

Propaganda Biased information which is presented in a way intended to persuade people of something, or win them over to a particular point of view.

Quill pen A pen made from the central tube (quill) of a feather.

Search engine A web site which keeps a very complex and full database of words that appear on web pages and allows you to search through this to find web pages about a particular topic.

Social networking The use of social media sites to keep in touch with and share files with a large number of people, usually for fun rather than business.

Sumer A place in the Middle East which was the site of the earliest known civilisation. It lies between two rivers, the Tigris and Euphrates, and is now part of southern Iraq.

Virtual Not real; simulated by a computer so as to seem realistic.

Virus A program which is deliberately introduced into a computer or network to steal information or to prevent it from working properly.

Wearable computer A piece of clothing or an accessory, such as a watch or wristband, that contains computer technology and can (usually) connect to the Internet.

Webcam A video or still camera which is connected to the Internet and feeds its images to a web page where people can view them as they occur.

Wiki A publicly sourced collection of information that builds into an online encyclopedia that anyone can use and add to.

Index

Top ways to stay safe online

You can have great fun on the Internet, but it also has its dangers. Keep yourself safe online by following these guidelines.

- When online, never reveal your real-world contact details, such as your full name, where you live or which school you go to.

- If anyone says anything to you online that you don't like, or if you see anything that makes you feel uncomfortable, tell a grown-up you can trust, such as a parent or a teacher.

- Don't post anything you might regret later, such as embarrassing photos or stories of stupid things you've done. Information spreads and hangs around for years online.

- Never post anything mean or embarrassing about anyone else – that's cyberbullying.

- Log out of all your accounts and pages before leaving the computer, so that other people can't use them as if they were you.

- Choose passwords that other people can't guess, and don't write them down where they can be recognised.

- Never agree to meet up with someone you only know online. Tell a grown-up if someone you know online asks to meet you. Remember that you don't really know who they are – it's easy to pretend online to be someone you're not.

Crazy Internet statistics

- There are nearly a billion active web sites on the Web.

- There are more than 10 billion Internet-connected devices (computers, tablets, phones and so on), but only 3 billion or so people in the world who use the Internet.

- Over 26,000 GB (gigabytes) of data are sent over the Internet every second.

- That mass of data includes 2.4 million emails sent every second, and most of that is 'spam' (junk email).

- One popular search engine hosts 173 million searches every hour.

- Internet 'rush hour' is between 7.00 and 9.00 p.m. in many countries. That's when people are home from work and school and have time to go online.

- 800 million Internet users speak English, and around 700 million speak Chinese. The next most common online languages are Spanish and Arabic, with 136 million each.

- The Internet changes so fast that some of the information on this page is bound to be out of date by the time you read it.

They've sent these pictures early to avoid the rush hour!

Did you know?

- No-one owns or runs the Web. Anyone at all can start a web site or a blog and post information online, and no-one is checking that it's true or accurate – so it's up to you to judge whether the sources you're using are reliable.

- About 10% of all the electricity we use in the world goes on using the Internet and keeping it going. But in many ways the Internet helps us save energy. So, is it good or bad for the environment? It's hard to tell!

- The oldest person known to have learned to use the Internet was Katherine Young (born Zheng Xun), who took a computing course at the age of 97 and used the Internet until her death at 104.

- The '@' character in email addresses is called 'little mouse' in Chinese, 'elephant's trunk' in Danish and Swedish, 'spider monkey' in German and 'snail' in Italian. In Hebrew it's 'strudel' and in Czech it's 'rollmops' (a rolled-up pickled herring).

- Language options available on one well-known search engine include Pirate, the science-fiction language Klingon, and Latin, the language of the ancient Romans.